Breaking Fr{  Relati

A Guide To Setting Boundaries and Moving On.

Published by Kate May

Copyright © 2024 Kate May

All Rights Reserved.

No part of this publication may be reproduced, distributed, or transmitted in any form or by any means, including photocopying, recording, or other electronic or mechanical methods, without the prior written permission of the publisher, except in the case of brief quotations embodied in critical reviews and certain other noncommercial uses permitted by copyright law.

For permission requests, write to the publisher, addressed "Attention: Permissions Coordinator," at the address:
katemay71@gmail.com

Table of Contents

Introduction - What is wrong with me? 11

   What is a toxic relationship? 17

   Recognising the signs of a toxic relationship...19

   The impact of toxic relationships on your mental health...20

   Boundaries 22

Chapter 2. Healing from a Toxic Relationship.....23

   Journaling 23

   Meditation..24

   Spend Time Outdoors 24

   Exercise At Home 24

   Read and Educate 24

   Creative Hobbies 24

   Listen To Music or Podcasts 25

   DIY Spa Day...25

   Declutter 25

   Connect With Loved Ones 25

   Processing the pain of a toxic relationship 26

   Seeking therapy and support 27

   Practicing self-care and self-love 28

Dealing with Emotional Manipulation................30

- **Develop Self-Awareness**.................................30
- **Set Clear Boundaries**......................................31
- **Stay Emotionally Detached**............................31
- **Think Critically**..31
- **Seek Outside Opinions**...................................32
- **Build Emotional Resilience**.............................32
- **Keep Records**...32
- **Stay Connected**..33
- **Communicate Assertively**..............................33
- **Know When To Walk Away**.............................33

Chapter 3. Setting Boundaries for a Healthy Future...34

- Identifying your values and boundaries..........34
- Communicating your boundaries effectively...36
- Enforcing your boundaries confidently...........38
- Understanding the 7 Types of Boundaries......40
- Emotional Boundaries......................................40
- Physical Boundaries...40
- Intellectual Boundaries....................................40
- Time Boundaries...40

Material Boundaries 40

Sexual Boundaries 41

Digital Boundaries 41

Common Mistakes 41

Establishing Healthy Boundaries 41

Here are 30 ideas of boundaries you might consider in your relationships: 42

Physical Boundaries 42

Emotional Boundaries 42

Time and Energy Boundaries 43

Communication Boundaries 43

Financial Boundaries 44

Social and Relationship Boundaries 44

Digital Boundaries 44

Additional Personal Boundaries 45

Personal Values 45

Why Are Personal Values Important? 45

They Guide Your Decisions 45

They Shape Your Character 46

They Give Your Life Meaning 46

They Help You Set Goals 46

They Improve Your Relationships 46

Examples of Personal Values 46

How Values Work in Real Life 47

To Identify Your Values, Think About: 47

Living Your Values 48

Personal Values Worksheet. 49

Step 1: Identify Your Values 49

Step 2. Prioritise Your Values 50

Step 3: Reflect on Your Values. 51

Step 4: Action Plan 52

Step 5: Review and Reflect 53

Personal Boundaries Worksheet. 53

Physical Boundaries 54

Emotional Boundaries 54

Time and Energy Boundaries 54

Communication Boundaries 55

Financial Boundaries 55

Social and Relationship Boundaries 56

Digital Boundaries 56

Additional Personal Boundaries 56

Chapter 4. Moving On and Thriving 57

Letting go of past resentments........................57

Embracing your independence and freedom ..58

Building healthy relationships in the future....59

Chapter 5. Preventing History from Repeating Itself..61

Reflecting on past relationships for growth 61

Setting boundaries early on in new relationships 62

Learning to trust your instincts and intuition ..63

Chapter 6. Embracing Your Power and Strength .65

Celebrating your journey to healing 65

Empowering yourself to live authentically 67

Inspiring other men and women to break free from toxic relationships 68

Chapter 7. Get Your Confidence Back................70

Chapter 8. 18 Traits of Toxic People 79

Manipulative..79

Constantly Negative.......................................80

Self-Centred 80

Criticising..80

Victim Mentality..81

Dishonesty 81

Jealous and Envious 82

Lack of Empathy 82

Controlling 82

Gossiping 83

Unreliable 83

Passive-Aggressive 83

Entitled 84

Excessive Drama 84

Inconsistent 84

Gaslighting 85

Narcissism 85

10 Common Narcissistic Traits 86

Emotional Abuse 88

Chapter 9. Leaving a Toxic Relationship 91

Emotional Manipulation and Financial Control. 92

Verbal and Physical Intimidation. 92

Stalking Behaviour and Refusal to Accept Breakup. 93

Chapter 10. Actionable Steps to Leave 93

Create a Comprehensive Safety Plan 93

- Build a Strong Support Network 94
- Document Everything Meticulously 95
- Protect Your Digital Presence and Privacy 96
- Plan and Execute Your Exit Strategy 97
- Long term planning 98

Chapter 11. Personal Stories of Overcoming Toxic Relationships..99

Chapter 12. Why Positive Affirmations Should Be Your Daily Superpower..................................102

Introduction - What is wrong with me?

"How on earth have I let this happen again? What the hell am I doing? I don't deserve to be treated like this by anyone."

"I just can't take anymore... I need to get away from him."

If you're like I used to be, this was a common conversation with myself. I always seemed to attract the wrong guy. It happened again and again. Sometimes it would end in domestic violence and that's not to mention the emotional and financial abuse that went with it. The list goes on.

Why was I always finding myself in the cycle of love, partnered with pain, disappointment and sometimes, enduring absolute hell?

Over the years I thought I had seen the last of the 'bad guy' as I had the knowledge, knew the red flags and I actually thought I was in control of how my life would turn out.

It seems that no matter how high my boundaries were set, the 'bad guy' would appear again. He was always nice at first. Funny, happy and, well basically the dream guy. Then the games started. The red flags flying everywhere but by then my heart had taken over my head and all boundaries and rules were out the window. Sound familiar?

I seemed to always be up against an inflated ego that craved constant attention. There was very little empathy. He often manipulated me through tactics like gaslighting and emotional blackmail. Always alternating between charm and criticism.

He never admitted he was wrong. Instead, he blamed me or others for everything and got angry when he thought anyone had insulted him, even if they hadn't.

His behaviour left me feeling confused, drained and questioning my self-worth. He often had a need for control and had an inability to form genuine emotional connections. He frequently lied. It was a case in which you just didn't know what to believe!

If you can relate to any of this, then you know exactly what I mean. It's not a place any man or woman should be in.

We enter into love relationships because we are drawn to the person. We love who they are and every aspect of them makes us happy. We should not go into a relationship with the mindset that they need to change. Over time, there will be things we dislike. The important thing is to remember that we fell in love with them for who they were when we first met. We are meant to evolve and mature together.

There is so much revealed to us along the way and the red flags and gut feelings are there for a reason. They are the warning signs that we need to act on.

A friend of mine once said, "If you think you need to change someone you're in the wrong relationship."

With the knowledge and experience I have now, I think this is true.

Adapting and growing together is part of the journey. We aren't meant to change who we are or who they are. It's about finding that sweet spot where we can be ourselves while still making room for each other. Sometimes it's messy and we might step on each other's toes but that's okay.

The key is to keep talking, keep listening and remember why we chose each other in the first place. It's not about moulding someone into our ideal partner. It's about appreciating them for who they are, flaws and all. If we can laugh about our oddities together, we're definitely on the right track!

A love relationship shouldn't feel like you're constantly walking on eggshells or second-guessing yourself. It shouldn't leave you drained, questioning your worth or feeling like you're never good enough.

Love isn't about control, manipulation or fear. It's not supposed to dim your light or make you feel small. A relationship shouldn't require you to sacrifice your dreams, your friendships or your sense of self. It's not meant to be a constant battle or a source of anxiety.

If you're always the one compromising or making excuses for your partner's behaviour, that's not love – that's a relationship that will never work. Real love lifts you up, it doesn't tear you down. Trust your gut – if something feels off, it probably is.

If you are currently in a toxic relationship or you have been in the past, this guide will help you to move on.

I've moved on and you can too.

Let me introduce myself. I'm Kate May, a life coach and therapist in my early 50's with a passion for helping others create lives they truly love. My journey has been quite the adventure - I've worn many hats over the years!

As the eldest of five kids, I learned early on about responsibility and caring for others. I'm proud to be a Mum and a nanna, cherishing every moment with my family.

My career path has been anything but ordinary. I started working in construction as a painter and decorator when I was just 16 and stuck with it for years. It taught me the value of hard work and perseverance, skills that have served me well in all areas of life.

Life hasn't always been smooth sailing. I've faced my share of challenges, including battling addiction.

My struggles led me to discover the power of personal development. As part of my recovery journey, I dove into studying how to create positive change and it transformed my life in ways I never imagined. As well as many others.

I'm passionate about sharing what I've learned. Whether it's through life coaching or therapy, I love helping others tap into their potential and overcome obstacles. I believe that with the right tools and support, anyone can build a life they're excited about.

My approach is all about keeping it real. I've been there, done that and I'm not afraid to share my experiences if they can help someone else.

So, if you're ready to shake things up and create some positive changes in your life, I'm here to support you every step of the way.

Chapter 1. Understanding Toxic Relationships

What is a toxic relationship?

A toxic relationship is one that is harmful, draining and ultimately detrimental to your well-being. It can come in many forms, whether it's emotional, physical or psychological abuse. Toxic relationships are characterised by manipulation, control and a lack of respect for boundaries. In these relationships, you may feel constantly on edge, anxious or unhappy.

If you have experienced heartbreak and are looking to set new boundaries to prevent history from repeating itself, identifying toxic relationships is crucial. It's important to recognise the signs early on so that you can protect yourself and your emotional well-being.

Some common signs of a toxic relationship include constant criticism, belittling or demeaning behaviour from your partner. They may try to control your every move, isolate you from friends and family or refuse to take responsibility for their actions. In a toxic relationship, communication is often one-sided, with one partner dominating the conversation and dismissing the other's feelings.

Setting boundaries when you're already in a toxic relationship can be difficult, but it is essential for your own mental and emotional health. It may involve establishing clear limits on what behaviour is acceptable, what is not and being willing to enforce those boundaries if they are crossed. It may also mean seeking support from friends, family or a therapist to help you navigate the complexities of a toxic relationship and find the strength to move on.

Breaking free from toxic relationships is a process, but it is possible with self- awareness, courage and a commitment to your personal well-being. I've dragged myself away from a few! By setting new boundaries and learning to recognise the signs of toxicity, you will gain the strength to protect yourself from further heartbreak. You can then set the bar and build healthier, more fulfilling relationships in the future.

Recognising the signs of a toxic relationship

Recognising the signs of a toxic relationship is the first step towards breaking free from its destructive cycle. As a woman who has experienced heartbreak and is looking to set new boundaries, it is crucial to be able to identify when a relationship is no longer serving you.

One of the key signs of a toxic relationship is when you constantly feel drained, anxious or unhappy in the presence of your partner. If you find yourself walking on eggshells, constantly trying to please them or avoid conflict, it's a red flag that the relationship is unhealthy. Trust your gut instincts - if something doesn't feel right, it probably isn't.

Another sign to watch out for is if your partner is controlling or manipulative. This can manifest in various ways, such as isolating you from friends and family, making decisions for you without your input or belittling your thoughts and feelings.

Healthy relationships are built on mutual respect and trust, so if you feel like you are being controlled or manipulated, it may be time to reevaluate the relationship.

If your partner consistently disrespects your boundaries, whether emotional, physical or personal, it is a clear indication of a toxic dynamic. Setting boundaries is essential for maintaining your self-respect and autonomy. If you have a partner and he disregards them, it is a sign of disrespect and lack of consideration for your well-being.

Recognising the signs of a toxic relationship is crucial. Trust your instincts, pay attention to how you feel in the relationship and don't ignore red flags. Setting boundaries and prioritising your well-being is key to breaking free from toxic relationships and moving towards a healthier, happier future.

The impact of toxic relationships on your mental health

Toxic relationships can have a huge negative impact on your mental health, often leaving lasting scars that are difficult to heal. It takes time but they do heal. Whether it's a romantic partner, family member, friend or colleague, being in a toxic relationship can lead to feelings of worthlessness, anxiety, depression and low self- esteem.

You may often find yourself constantly second-guessing your own thoughts and feelings. Feeling like you're walking on eggshells to avoid conflict and sacrificing your own needs and desires to keep the peace. These patterns of behaviour can take a significant toll on your mental health, leading to chronic stress, feelings of isolation and a sense of powerlessness.

It's important to recognise the signs and take steps to protect your mental health. This may involve ending the relationship altogether. As hard as it may seem now, it's the only answer if resolutions can't be implemented. Heavy on the heart and mind but your happiness is paramount.

Setting boundaries is essential as it allows you to protect themselves from further harm and regain a sense of control over your life. By establishing boundaries, you can communicate your needs and expectations clearly, assert your own values and beliefs and create a safe space for you to heal and grow.

Moving on can be challenging, but with the right support and tools, you can break free from the cycle of toxicity and create a healthier, more fulfilling life.. By setting new boundaries and prioritising your mental health, you can ensure that history does not repeat itself and that you can move forward with confidence.

Boundaries

Boundaries are the limits and rules you set for yourself in relationships to protect your well-being and personal space. They help define what you're comfortable with and how you expect others to treat you. Setting boundaries ensures that interactions are respectful and that your needs are recognised and valued. For example, saying "no" when you don't want to do something or asking someone to speak to you in a more respectful tone, are ways of establishing healthy boundaries.

Chapter 2. Healing from a Toxic Relationship

Healing from a toxic relationship is a deeply personal journey that requires time, patience and most importantly, self-care.

As a therapist, I've seen countless women emerge stronger and more resilient after prioritising their well-being. Self-care isn't just about pampering yourself and nurturing your mind, body and spirit. It's vital in reclaiming your life and building a healthier, happier future.

Here are ten easy-to-incorporate self-care strategies to help you on your healing journey. New habits for a stronger you.

Journaling

Take a few minutes every day to write down your thoughts, feelings, and reflections. This can help you process emotions and gain clarity.

Meditation

Practice guided meditation using free apps like Headspace or find a free meditation on YouTube. Even a few minutes of deep breathing can reduce stress.

Spend Time Outdoors

A walk in a nearby park, a hike with friends or just sitting in your garden. Nature has a calming effect on the mind.

Exercise At Home

Engage in physical exercise at home with free workout videos on platforms like YouTube. Yoga, Pilates or body weight exercises.

Read and Educate

Read books, articles or blogs that interest you. I don't mean scrolling through Instagram or Facebook regularly.

Creative Hobbies

Engage in creative activities such as drawing, painting or writing. Revamp an old piece of furniture with furniture paint. Creativity can be a great outlet for stress.

Listen To Music or Podcasts

Create a playlist of your favourite songs or listen to inspiring and uplifting podcasts. Music and spoken word can be very therapeutic.

DIY Spa Day

Pamper yourself with a DIY spa day at home. Take a long bath, use a face mask and give yourself a manicure or pedicure.

Declutter

Spend some time decluttering and organising a space in your home. A tidy environment can promote a sense of calm and order.

Connect With Loved Ones

Reach out to friends or family members for a chat, whether through a phone call, video call or text. Meaningful connections will provide emotional support and boost your mood.

Processing the pain of a toxic relationship

Processing the pain of a toxic relationship can be a difficult and challenging experience for anyone. It's important to acknowledge and validate your feelings, as well as give yourself the time and space to heal.

One of the first steps in processing the pain of a toxic relationship is to allow yourself to feel all of the emotions that come with it. This may include anger, sadness, betrayal, and even relief. It's important to remember that all of these emotions are valid and part of the healing process.

It's important to identify what behaviour is acceptable to you and what is not and communicate those boundaries to the people in your life. This can help prevent history from repeating itself and protect you from falling into similar toxic patterns in the future.

Practising self-care and self-love is essential in processing the pain of a toxic relationship. Take time to do things that bring you joy, whether it's spending time with loved ones, engaging in a hobby or practising mindfulness and self-reflection.

Remember, it's okay to grieve the loss of a toxic relationship and take the time you need to heal. By processing the pain and setting new boundaries, you can break free and move forward with strength.

Seeking therapy and support

After experiencing a toxic relationship, it is common to have feelings of confusion, self-doubt and emotional pain. Ensure you find a safe space to explore and process these difficult emotions either alone or with a friend or family member.

Therapy can help you gain insight into the patterns and dynamics of toxic relationships, allowing you to understand why you may have been drawn to such relationships in the past. It will help you to identify and challenge negative beliefs about yourself.

In therapy, you can learn healthy coping mechanisms and communication skills that will empower you to gain strength and set new boundaries in future relationships.

By setting clear boundaries and communicating your needs effectively, you can protect yourself from falling into the same toxic patterns. It's easily done.

If at any point of your journey, you feel that therapy would be a positive way forward for you, I offer online sessions. So, wherever you are in the world, we can book a time that suits. Visit cheltenham-hypnotherapy.com to book a free call.

I don't like the word 'therapy' but it's an act of self-care and self-love. A courageous step towards breaking free and creating a happier, more fulfilling life. By investing in your emotional well-being and growth, you can set yourself to walk on a path of healing and empowerment. Often, just one session can put you on the right path.

Practicing self-care and self-love

One of the first steps in practising self-care is to acknowledge your worth and value as a person. Remind yourself that you deserve love, respect and happiness in your life. Take the time to reflect on the qualities that make you unique and special and embrace them wholeheartedly.

Self-love involves treating yourself with kindness and compassion, just as you would a close friend. Practice positive affirmations daily, reminding yourself of your strengths and capabilities. I've given you a list of examples at the end of this book. Engage in activities that bring you joy and fulfilment, whether it's spending time with loved ones, pursuing a hobby or simply taking time for yourself to relax and recharge.

Learn to recognise toxic behaviour and relationships and don't be afraid to distance yourself from them. Communicate your needs and expectations to others and don't hesitate to assert yourself when necessary.

By practising self-care and self-love, you are taking the necessary steps to heal and move on from past heartbreak. Remember that you are deserving of happiness and fulfilment and that setting boundaries is a powerful way to ensure that history does not repeat itself. Embrace your worth and value and prioritise your well-being above all else. You matter.

Dealing with Emotional Manipulation.

Emotional manipulation is a subtle yet powerful tactic that can undermine your confidence and well-being. It often goes unnoticed until the damage is done. I found this to be a constant in all my toxic relationships. I've listed some tips to help you recognise, resist and overcome emotional manipulation. You must protect your emotional health and maintain control over your interactions. These strategies will empower you to navigate manipulative situations with confidence and clarity.

Develop Self-Awareness

Understanding your own emotions is the first step in defending yourself against manipulation. Pay attention to your feelings and reactions in different situations. Knowing why you feel a certain way can help you distinguish between your genuine emotions and those influenced by someone else.

Set Clear Boundaries

Boundaries are essential in any relationship. Clearly define what you find acceptable and unacceptable. Communicate your limits assertively and stick to them. Manipulators take advantage of confusion so clear communication is your best defence.

Stay Emotionally Detached

When you're dealing with a manipulator, try to keep your emotions in check. This doesn't mean you should become cold or unfeeling, just approach the situation with a level head. Emotional distance allows you to see things more objectively and reduces the manipulator's influence over you. Silence is a great way to respond.

Think Critically

Enhance your critical thinking skills to analyse the manipulator's words and actions. Ask yourself what their true intentions might be and look for evidence to back up their claims. A sceptical and questioning attitude can protect you from falling for manipulative tactics.

Seek Outside Opinions

Talk to friends, family or a friend about your situation. They might be able to provide an outside perspective that you might not have considered. Sometimes, others can see manipulation tactics that are hard to recognise when you're directly involved.

Build Emotional Resilience

Work on strengthening your emotional resilience through self-care practices, mindfulness and if necessary, professional therapy. A resilient mindset helps you recover quickly from emotional manipulation and maintain your inner strength. Try to ignore the comments made. Silently call them a name and tell yourself that whatever they say about you is a load of rubbish!

Keep Records

Document your interactions with the manipulator. This can include notes on conversations, behaviours and incidents. Having a written record helps you stay grounded in reality and provides concrete evidence if the manipulator tries to twist the truth. Use a journal if you have somewhere you can keep it private or use a Google document.

Stay Connected

Isolation is a common tactic used by manipulators. Keep in touch with a supportive network of friends and family. Regular social interactions can provide you with emotional support and perspective, making it harder for a manipulator to control you. Do not isolate yourself. Get away for a few days if you can. You may not feel like it but it will do you the world of good.

Communicate Assertively

When expressing your needs and boundaries, use assertive communication. Speak clearly and use "I" statements to convey your feelings without blaming others. This approach helps you stay in control of the conversation and strengthens your position.

Know When To Walk Away

Sometimes, the best solution is to distance yourself from the manipulator. If their behaviour doesn't change despite your efforts, it might be necessary to reduce or eliminate contact to protect your well-being. It's most likely time to walk away.

Dealing with emotional manipulation requires a combination of self-awareness, boundary-setting and resilience. By applying these tips, you can work your way through manipulative situations more effectively and safeguard your emotional health. Your well-being comes first and it's okay to prioritise your peace and happiness. In fact, its a must.

Chapter 3. Setting Boundaries for a Healthy Future

Identifying your values and boundaries

Understanding what is truly important to you and what you will and will not tolerate in a relationship is crucial for setting healthy boundaries and preventing history from repeating itself.

Identifying your values means taking the time to reflect on what matters most to you in life. This could include things like honesty, respect, trust and communication. When you're clear on your values, you can use them as a guide for how you want to be treated in a relationship.

Setting boundaries is about knowing your limits and communicating them effectively to others. This could involve establishing boundaries around how you want to be treated, what behaviours are unacceptable to you and what consequences will occur if those boundaries are crossed. It is important to remember that setting boundaries is not about controlling others, but rather about taking care of yourself and your well-being.

When identifying your values and boundaries, it is important to be honest with yourself about what you need and deserve in a relationship. It can be helpful to seek support from friends and family to help you clarify your values and set boundaries that are healthy and empowering for you.

By identifying your values and boundaries, you'll create a strong foundation for setting new boundaries in your relationships and breaking free from toxic patterns. Remember, you deserve to be treated with respect and kindness and by setting clear boundaries, you can create the space for healthy and fulfilling relationships to flourish.

Communicating your boundaries effectively

Communicating your boundaries effectively is essential in any relationship, but especially so after experiencing heartbreak. It's a way to protect yourself from toxic behaviour and ensure that history doesn't repeat itself. You might struggle with clearly expressing your needs and limits but it is essential to learn how to do this in order to move on.

One primary aspect of communicating boundaries effectively is being assertive. You need to state your needs and limits in a clear and direct manner, without being aggressive or passive. Practice using "I" statements to express how you feel and what you need from the other person. For example, instead of saying, 'You always make me feel sad,' Try saying, 'I feel hurt when you speak to me that way.'

Avoid Over-Explaining When setting boundaries, it's crucial to avoid over-explaining or justifying yourself. Over-explaining often stems from a need to be taken seriously, but it can come across as a lack of confidence or insecurity. Instead, communicate your boundaries with clarity and confidence, without feeling the need to justify them. Keep your message simple and straightforward.

It's also important to set consequences for when your boundaries are crossed. Let the other person know what will happen if they continue to disregard your limits.

This could be as simple as leaving the situation or ending the conversation. By setting consequences, you are showing that you are serious about your boundaries and expect them to be respected.

Setting boundaries is not about controlling the other person's behaviour. It's about taking care of yourself and your personal well-being. It's okay to say 'No' and prioritise your needs. Practice self-care and surround yourself with supportive people who respect your boundaries. By communicating your boundaries effectively, you stand your ground and you'll create healthier connections in the future.

Enforcing your boundaries confidently

One key aspect of enforcing your boundaries confidently is to first identify what your boundaries are. Take some time to reflect on your past relationships and consider what behaviours and actions are unacceptable to you. Once you have a clear understanding of your boundaries, communicate them assertively to others. Remember, you have the right to prioritise your own needs, You are not a door mat. You want to be treated just as you treat others.

If you feel disrespected, use your voice to let the person know that it is not acceptable.

It is important to remain firm and consistent. Do not let others guilt-trip you or manipulate you into compromising your boundaries. Stand your ground and be assertive in communicating your needs and expectations. You are the writer of your own story. Write a an amazing one!

Surround yourself with supportive friends and loved ones who respect your boundaries and uplift you. Engage in activities that bring you joy and fulfillment and prioritise your own well-being above everything else. You may think it's selfish. Its not selfish. You always come first. If you don't put yourself first, you'll be no good at being available to others.

Enforcing your boundaries confidently may not always be easy, especially if you have a history of toxic relationships or you're still in one. Remember, you deserve to be treated with respect and kindness and enforcing your boundaries confidently is a powerful step towards reclaiming your self-worth and rebuilding your life.

If you don't feel confident about it, practice having conversations. eg: "I won't be spoken to like that." "There's no need to be so nasty". "I'm perfectly happy with who I am thank you."

Understanding the 7 Types of Boundaries

Emotional Boundaries

Manage your emotions and respect others' feelings. - Example: Telling a friend you're uncomfortable discussing personal issues

Physical Boundaries

Define personal space and touch. - Example: Politely refusing hugs if you're uncomfortable.

Intellectual Boundaries

Respect different opinions and ideas. - Example: Sharing your views while being open to others perspectives.

Time Boundaries

Prioritise your time and energy. - Example: Setting specific times for work and personal activities.

Material Boundaries

Manage possessions and finances. - Example: Setting rules about borrowing personal items.

Sexual Boundaries

Establish comfort levels and consent in sexual activities. - Example: Communicating your limits with a partner.

Digital Boundaries

Govern your online presence and privacy. - Example: Setting social media privacy settings.

Common Mistakes

Boundaries are not selfish or rude; they are about self-care and respect.They do not control others but define how you want to be treated. Boundaries can adapt over time and are essential even in close relationships. Saying "no" is part of setting boundaries.

Establishing Healthy Boundaries

Identify your needs and limits.

Communicate assertively using "I" statements.

Avoid over-explaining.

Be consistent.

Practice self-care.

Here are 30 ideas of boundaries you might consider in your relationships:

Check the ones you feel are important to you and add any additional boundaries you'd like to set in the blank spaces provided.

Physical Boundaries

I have the right to say no to physical touch at any time.

My personal space must be respected.

I decide when and if I want to be intimate.

My body is my own and make decisions about it.

I choose how and when to express physical affection.

Emotional Boundaries

I'm entitled to my own feelings and emotions.

I don't have to take responsibility for others' emotions.

I can express my feelings without fear of retaliation.

I have the right to privacy in my thoughts and feelings.

I don't have to share everything I think or feel.

Time and Energy Boundaries

I can say no to requests without feeling guilty.

My time is valuable and I choose how to spend it.

I have the right to rest and recharge.

I don't have to be available 24/7.

I can prioritise self-care without feeling selfish.

Communication Boundaries

I deserve to be spoken to with respect.

I have the right to express my opinions and ideas.

I can ask for what I need directly.

I don't have to engage in arguments or debates I don't want to.

I can end conversations that make me uncomfortable.

Financial Boundaries

I have control over my own money and financial decisions.

I don't have to disclose my financial information if I don't want to.

I can say no to lending money or making purchases I'm not comfortable with.

Social and Relationship Boundaries

I can choose my own friends and maintain those relationships.

I have the right to spend time alone or with others as I choose.

I don't have to attend every social event I'm invited to.

I can end relationships that are unhealthy or no longer serve me.

Digital Boundaries

I have the right to privacy in my online activities and communications.

I can choose what I share on social media.

I don't have to respond immediately to messages or calls.

Additional Personal Boundaries

Personal Values

Personal values are the core beliefs and principles that guide your life. They're like your inner compass, helping you make decisions and choose how to behave.

Values are what you consider important and worthwhile in life.

Why Are Personal Values Important?

They Guide Your Decisions

Values help you make choices, big and small. When you're clear about what matters most to you, it's easier to decide what to do in different situations.

They Shape Your Character

Your values define who you are. They influence your personality and how you interact with others.

They Give Your Life Meaning

When you live according to your values, life feels more purposeful and satisfying

They Help You Set Goals

Values can help you figure out what you want to achieve in life, both personally and professionally.

They Improve Your Relationships

Understanding your values helps you connect with like-minded people and navigate differences with others.

Examples of Personal Values

Honesty: Always telling the truth and being sincere

Kindness: Treating others with compassion and consideration

Courage: Facing challenges and fears head-on

Growth: Continuously learning and improving yourself

Family: Prioritising and nurturing family relationships

How Values Work in Real Life

Imagine you value honesty. When faced with a situation where you could lie to avoid trouble, your value of honesty would encourage you to tell the truth, even if it's difficult.

Or, if you value personal growth, you might choose to take on new challenges at work or learn new skills in your free time, even when it's uncomfortable.

To Identify Your Values, Think About:

What's most important to you in life?

What makes you feel proud?

What do you stand for?

What behaviours do you admire in others?

Your values can change over time as you grow and have new experiences. It's good to reflect on them regularly.

Living Your Values

Once you know your values, try to make choices that align with them. This might mean saying '**NO**' to things that go against your values or actively seeking out opportunities that support them.

Living in line with your values can lead to greater happiness, self-esteem and a sense of authenticity in your life. Personal values are your life's foundation. They guide your actions, shape your character and help you create a life that feels meaningful and true to who you are.

Personal values are your life's foundation. They guide your actions, shape your character and help you create a life that feels meaningful and true to who you are.

Personal Values Worksheet.

Personal values guide our behaviour and decisions, reflecting what is most important to you. This worksheet will help you identify and prioritise your core values.

Step 1: Identify Your Values

Here is a list of common personal vales, Circle or highlight the ones that resonate most with you.

Family	Compassion
Friendship	Creativity
Community	Achievement
Respect	Financial Stability
Spirituality	Adventure
Security	Learning
Love	Honesty
Joy	Integrity
Empathy	Respect
Growth	Independence
Health	

Step 2. Prioritise Your Values

Select your top ten values from the list above and rank them in order of importance.

1.
2.
3.
4.
5.
6.
7.
8.
9.
10.

Step 3: Reflect on Your Values.

Answer the following questions to gain deeper insight into your values.

Why are these values important to you?

- ☐
- ☐
- ☐
- ☐
- ☐

How do these values influence your daily decisions and actions?

-
-
-
-
-

Are there any areas of your life where you feel your values are not being honoured? How can you address this?

-
-
-
-
-

How can you incorporate your top values into your daily life?

-
-
-
-
-

Step 4: Action Plan

Develop a plan to align your lifestyle more closely with your values.

Value:
Action:
Timeline:

Value:
Action:
Timeline:

Value:
Action:
Timeline:

Step 5: Review and Reflect

Periodically review this worksheet to reflect on your values and make adjustments as needed. Revisit the action plan to ensure you are staying aligned with your core values.

Personal Boundaries Worksheet.

Here are 30 ideas for boundaries you might consider setting in your relationships:

Review the following boundary ideas. Check the ones you feel are important to you and add any additional boundaries you'd like to set in the blank spaces provided.

Physical Boundaries

I have the right to say no to physical touch at any time.

My personal space must be respected.

I decide when and if I want to be intimate.

My body is my own and I make decisions about it.

I choose how and when to express physical affection

Emotional Boundaries

I'm entitled to my own feelings and emotions.

I don't have to take responsibility for others' emotions.

I can express my feelings without fear of retaliation.

I have the right to privacy in my thoughts and feelings.

I don't have to share everything I think or feel.

Time and Energy Boundaries

I can say no to requests without feeling guilty.

My time is valuable and I choose how to spend it.

I have the right to rest and recharge.

I don't have to be available 24/7.

I can prioritise self-care without feeling selfish.

Communication Boundaries

I deserve to be spoken to with respect.

I have the right to express my opinions and ideas.

I can ask for what I need directly.

I don't have to engage in arguments or debates I don't want to.

I can end conversations that make me uncomfortable.

Financial Boundaries

I have control over my own money and financial decisions.

I don't have to disclose my financial information if I don't want to.

I can say no to lending money or making purchases I'm not comfortable with.

Social and Relationship Boundaries

I can choose my own friends and maintain those relationships.

I have the right to spend time alone or with others as I choose.

I don't have to attend every social event I'm invited to.

I can end relationships that are unhealthy or no longer serve me.

Digital Boundaries

I have the right to privacy in my online activities and communications.

I can choose what I share on social media.

I don't have to respond immediately to messages or calls.

Additional Personal Boundaries

Setting and maintaining boundaries is an important part of self-care and healthy relationships.

It's okay to adjust your boundaries as needed and communicate them clearly to others at any point in your relationships with anyone.

Chapter 4. Moving On and Thriving

Letting go of past resentments

It can be easy to hold onto feelings of anger, hurt and betrayal from past relationships. However, holding onto these negative emotions only holds you back from healing and moving forward.

When you hold onto past resentments, you allow the toxic energy of those relationships to continue to have power over you. It is important to recognise that by letting go of these resentments, you are not excusing the behaviour of your past partners. Instead, you are choosing to release yourself from the burden of carrying around negative emotions that no longer serve you.

One powerful way to let go of past resentments is through forgiveness. Forgiveness is not about condoning the actions of others, it's about freeing yourself from the pain and anger that you have been holding onto. By forgiving those who have wronged you, you will be able to release yourself from the emotional baggage that has been weighing you down. You don't want to be carrying that around with you.

Letting go of past resentments is essential. By forgiving those who have hurt you and setting new boundaries in your relationships, you can break free from toxic patterns and move on to a brighter future. Remember, you deserve to be treated with love, respect, and kindness – both by others and by yourself.

If you're finding it hard to let go, write a letter to the person. Do not send it. Burn it. This really does help to let go.

Embracing your independence and freedom

After experiencing a toxic relationship, it can be easy to feel lost and unsure of yourself. Embrace your independence and avoid falling into the same patterns in future relationships. You're free again. That's something to celebrate even if it doesn't feel like it at the time.

Embracing your independence means taking the time to focus on yourself and your own needs. This may involve rediscovering old hobbies or passions, spending time with friends and family or simply taking some time to reflect on your own values and priorities.

By taking the time to nurture your own sense of self, you will be better equipped to set healthy boundaries in future relationships.

By embracing your independence and freedom, you are taking the first steps towards setting yourself up for healthier, more fulfilling connections in the future. You deserve to be treated with respect and kindness and by prioritising your own well-being, you are setting the stage for a fantastic future. A future that will put a rather large smile on your face!

Building healthy relationships in the future

One of the first steps in building healthy relationships in the future is to reflect on past experiences and identify patterns that led to toxic relationships. By understanding the red flags and warning signs, you can make better choices in the future and avoid falling into the same traps. Don't forget to take time to heal from past heartbreak and work on self-love and self-care before entering into a new relationship. You need time to heal and regain your confidence.

You must communicate your needs and expectations clearly from the very start. Stand firm in enforcing your boundaries. This will mean saying 'No' to things that make you uncomfortable or it may mean you will have to walk away from new relationships that do not serve you. Remember, you deserve to be treated with respect and kindness in all of your relationships.

Build a strong support system of people that will help you navigate the challenges of dating and relationships and provide you with the love and encouragement you need to thrive.

By taking these steps to build healthy relationships in the future, you will create a life filled with love, respect and joy. You deserve nothing less than the best in all of your relationships.

Chapter 5. Preventing History from Repeating Itself

Reflecting on past relationships for growth

Reflecting on past relationships allows you to learn valuable lessons and identify patterns to ensure history does not repeat itself.

It's natural to want to move on quickly after a heartbreak. However, taking the time to reflect on what went wrong in your past relationships is a must for personal growth and healing. By looking back on past experiences, you can gain an insight into your own behaviours, triggers and the red flags that you may have overlooked in the past.

Reflecting, will help you to identify patterns that may be harmful to your mental and emotional well-being. Once you've made a note of them you can take proactive steps to break free from toxic cycles and create healthier relationships in the future.

Where were your boundaries crossed? Did you neglect to set boundaries altogether?

Write this stuff down. Take your time and reflect back on them.

Do this and you'll learn so much about yourself, Maybe you were too giving. Too thoughtful. Too bloody kind. You may have given too much from the onset. Learn to hold back and be distant sometimes. Create a life you love first, Don't always be available when they want to see you. At the first sight of a red flag, you can start to lay the laws down.

Setting boundaries early on in new relationships

When entering a new relationship, it can be easy to get caught up in the excitement and overlook red flags or warning signs. However, you must set the tone for how you expect to be treated.

One of the first steps in setting boundaries is knowing your worth and what you will not tolerate. What were the behaviours or actions that caused you pain or discomfort? Use these experiences as a guide for establishing boundaries in a new relationship.

Communicate openly and honestly with your new partner or friend about your boundaries. Let them know what is important to you and what behaviours are unacceptable. Boundaries are not about control. They are about respecting yourself and your needs.

Be firm in enforcing them and do not be afraid to walk away from a relationship that doesn't honour them. Your well-being should always come first and it's okay to prioritise yourself over a potentially toxic relationship. Look where it got you last time. Don't let your heart rule your head.

Trust yourself and your instincts and **do not** settle for anything less than you deserve. Break free from toxic patterns and create a new, healthy relationship dynamic that respects and honours you as a human being.

Learning to trust your instincts and intuition

It can be easy to doubt your own judgment and second-guess your decisions. Learning to trust your instincts and intuition is a must. If it doesn't feel right it probably isn't. We all know that, only sometimes we just hope that we're wrong. Especially if our heart is ruling our head.

Your instincts and intuition are powerful tools that can guide you in making the right decisions for yourself. They are often the first warning signs that something is not right in a relationship. You must listen to them. If something feels off or your intuition is telling you that a person is not good for you, trust that feeling and take action to protect yourself. If you think someone is lying, they probably are.

Trusting your instincts and intuition also means trusting yourself. You are the expert on your own life and experiences. You know what is best for you. By listening to your inner voice and following your intuition, you can avoid heartache in the future.

To strengthen your ability to trust your instincts and intuition, practice mindfulness and self-awareness. Pay attention to how you feel in different situations and with different people. Trust yourself to make the right decisions for yourself and remember that you deserve to be in healthy, loving relationships.

Trust yourself, listen to your inner voice, and know that you have the power to create the healthy, fulfilling relationships you deserve. Embrace your strengths and stay true to your values. Each step forward brings you closer to the happiness you seek and so deserve.

Chapter 6. Embracing Your Power and Strength

Celebrating your journey to healing

In your healing journey, take the time to celebrate your progress and growth. It is not an easy path to walk, but every step you take towards healing and setting boundaries is a victory worth acknowledging and celebrating.

It can be easy to focus on the pain and the past. You walked away from it. That in itself is a huge achievement. The pain is immense and it's such a hard thing to do. Start to recognise the strength and resilience it took for you to walk away.

If they left you, you're blessed. It may not feel like it but you're well rid of seriously bad rubbish.

Celebrating your journey to healing can take many forms. It could be as simple as treating yourself to a relaxing spa day or a night out with friends to toast to your progress and freedom. It could also involve reflecting on how far you have come and acknowledging the courage it took.

By celebrating your journey to healing, you are affirming to yourself that you are worthy of love, respect and healthy relationships. You are showing yourself that you have the power to create a brighter future for yourself, free from toxic influences and repeating patterns of the past.

Healing is not a quick and easy process and there may be setbacks along the way. Make sure that you celebrate your progress and victories, you are building resilience and self-compassion that will help you navigate any challenges that come your way.

So, take the time to honour and celebrate your journey. You deserve it and you are worth it. Keep moving forward, setting boundaries and prioritising your well-being. The best is yet to come.

Empowering yourself to live authentically

Empowering yourself to live authentically is a crucial step in breaking free. Recognise the power that you have within yourself.

Living authentically means honoring your values, beliefs and desires without compromising them for the sake of others. It requires self-awareness, self- acceptance and the courage to stand up for yourself and what you believe in.

By empowering yourself to live authentically, you are reclaiming your sense of self- worth and taking control of your own happiness.

Setting new boundaries is a key aspect of living authentically after experiencing heartbreak. It involves clearly communicating your needs, expectations and limits to others and not being afraid to enforce them. By setting boundaries, you are protecting yourself from toxic influences and creating a safe space for yourself to grow and heal.

In order to empower yourself to live authentically, it is important to engage in self-care practices that nurture your mind, body, and soul. This could involve therapy, meditation, exercise or spending time with loved ones who support and uplift you. By taking care of yourself, you are strengthening your sense of self and building the confidence to live your life on your own terms. Keep yourself busy.

Remember, you have the power to create the life you deserve. By empowering yourself to live authentically and set new boundaries, you are taking a crucial step towards breaking free from toxic relationships and moving on to a brighter, more fulfilling future.

Inspiring other men and women to break free from toxic relationships

As men and women who have experienced the pain and turmoil of toxic relationships, we have an opportunity to support and uplift one another.

One of the most powerful ways we can inspire other people is by sharing our own stories of survival and resilience. By opening up about our experiences we can let others know that they are not alone and that there is hope for a brighter future.

When we speak out about the ways in which we have set boundaries and moved on from toxic relationships, we show others that it is possible to break free from the cycle of abuse and manipulation.

By living our lives with strength, confidence, courage and self-love, we show other women that they too can find the strength within themselves to set boundaries and move on. When we prioritise our own well-being and happiness, we demonstrate to others that they deserve nothing less than to be treated with love and respect.

By inspiring others to break free from toxic relationships, we create a ripple effect of healing and empowerment that has the potential to transform lives.

Conversations with others, even strangers on a train or a bus can plant seeds. You give someone the knowledge, an example, a tip or a little hope and they walk away with that. Even if that seed doesn't grow for weeks or years to come, it will grow and you did that!

Chapter 7. Get Your Confidence Back

Emerging from a toxic relationship can leave you feeling vulnerable, diminished and unsure. Regaining your confidence is both possible and empowering.

Getting your confidence back is part of the new journey so you can rediscover your self-worth and inner strength.

By rebuilding your confidence, you not only heal those wounds but also empower yourself to make better choices and embrace the love and respect you truly deserve.

Try this list of examples on the next few pages to make a start in feeling good about yourself again!

Practice self-care - Take a relaxing bath or get a massage to show yourself some love. Get a haircut. Little things make all the difference.

Set small and achievable goals: Complete a short online course to build competence. There are lots of free courses out there or cheap ones on

Udemy. Write a weekly blog. Cut out sugar or alcohol. Small steps work wonders for your confidence.

Exercise regularly: Join a class to boost endorphins and your body image. Use an online app like 7M. Make it a habit.

Dress in clothes that make you feel good: Wear that outfit that always gets you compliments. Dress to impress yourself and don't keep that perfume/aftershave for special nights out. Wear it every day! I wear mine on building sites that I work at! It makes ME feel good.

Learn a new skill: Take up photography to challenge yourself and gain a sense of accomplishment. Post you images to Instagram. Try some form of art or learn a new trade online. There are lots of options.

Practice positive self-talk: Replace "I can't" with "I'll try my best" when facing challenges. You'll find lots of affirmations at the end of this book. Make it a daily habit.

Celebrate your achievements: No matter how small your achievement. Its a milestone. A mountain climbed. Treat yourself to your favourite dinner after hitting any of the above milestones. Buy a new top, a new lipstick or nail varnish. Treat yourself.

Surround yourself with supportive people: Have coffee with a friend who always lifts your spirits. Visit family.

Keep a gratitude journal: Write down three things you're grateful for each day. If you can't leave a journal lying around, voice your gratitude list out loud whilst you drive to work or just say them in your head. Gratitude is a wonderful habit to have.

Face a fear: Speak up in a meeting if you usually stay quiet. If you're not happy about something, speak up. You have a right to an opinion. Say 'NO', if you don't want to do something. You are in charge of you. Use your voice.

Volunteer: Help at a local animal shelter or second-hand shop to gain perspective and feel valuable. I did this for 10 years. It was like therapy to me. I love that role more than any of the other jobs I ever did.

Declutter your space: Organise your wardrobe to create a sense of control and fresh start. Empty those drawers full of bits and bobs you probably won't ever need. Make room for better things to come into your life. Less is more.

Practice saying NO: Decline an invitation to an event you don't really want to attend. If someone asks you to do something you don't have time for simply say, 'Sorry, I can't help you right now. Ask me another time.' Once you get the first 'NO' out of the way, it gets easier!

Seek therapy or counselling: Talk through your confidence issues with a professional if you can't find free talking therapy with someone close. Get it off your chest! Sometimes all someone needs is to be heard. to be listened to. I get people come to me for therapy and all they really needed was a long chat. They needed to be listened to.

Take social media breaks: Spend a weekend offline to reduce comparison to others and increase self-focus. Social media can make you more down and less confident. Take a break.

Try power posing: Stand like Wonder Woman or Superman for two minutes before an important event or before you have that conversation you've been meaning to have with someone for ages. Take a few deep breaths and boom! You're the bomb!

Develop a new hobby: A good example is gardening. You grow from seed and nurture that plant. There's nothing better than reaping the fruits of your own labour!

Practice self-compassion: Talk to yourself as you would a best friend when they've made a mistake or put themselves down.

Set boundaries: Tell a friend you can't always be available at short notice. Don't always answer your phone. Stop being available all the time. Time is precious and so are you.

Embrace your uniqueness: Make a list of your quirks and celebrate what makes you different.

Mirror work: Learn to love who you are. Every time you walk past a mirror and no ones watching, blow yourself a kiss. Sounds weird but eventually you'll be smiling back at yourself

Here are a few questions you could take the time to answer to get you on your way to a new and more confident you. Let's dive in and boost that confidence.

List 3 things that you're proud of accomplishing:

1.
2.
3.

What's one small thing you can do today to make yourself feel good?

1.

Write down 3 positive affirmations that resonate with you:

I am ...

I can ...

I deserve ...

1.

Who are 2 people in your life that make you feel loved and valued?

1.
2.

What's a skill or habit you have that you'd like to develop further?

1.
2.
3.

Describe a time when you overcame a challenge?

☐
☐

How did it make you feel?

☐
☐

What's one thing you'd like to try but have been afraid to?

What's holding you back?

When was the last time you felt truly proud of yourself and what led to that feeling?

If your closest friend described your best qualities, what do you think they would say?

What's one challenge you've overcome in the past that initially seemed daunting?

☐

By answering these question's you can reflect on your past achievements, your qualities and the challenges you have overcome. Recognise your capabilities and resilience

Time to remove the self-doubt and negative thinking. It's time to start writing the next chapter in your life. One full of confidence

Building confidence is a journey, not a destination. Be kind to yourself, celebrate small wins and keep pushing forward

Chapter 8. 18 Traits of Toxic People

Toxic people can have a harmful effect on your mental and emotional well-being. Recognising their traits can help you stay safe. I've listed 18 common traits of toxic individuals below, along with examples to explain each one

Manipulative

Toxic people often twist situations and words to their advantage. They might guilt- trip you into doing things you don't want to do. For example, a manipulative partner might say, "If you really cared about me, you would skip your plans so you could find the time to help me out.

Constantly Negative

These individuals always find something to complain about and often focus on the worst-case scenario. For example, during a team project, a toxic colleague might constantly point out previous and potential failures instead of contributing solutions. They might also single you out giving negative feedback for anything you might input. They might point out failures you may have had.

Self-Centred

Toxic people tend to be preoccupied with their own needs and desires. It's all about them and only them. They are hard-wired to ignore other people's feelings. A self- centred person might monopolise conversations, only talking about their achievements without showing any interest whatsoever in anyone else's lives.

Criticising

They frequently criticise and belittle others to make themselves feel superior. For instance, a toxic sister might constantly mock your career choices or personal decisions, undermining your confidence. Always adding to the conversation with how well they have done over the years

Victim Mentality

These individuals often see themselves as perpetual victims, blaming others for their problems. A partner with a victim mentality might refuse to take responsibility for their actions, claiming that life is always unfair to them. It's always someone else's fault. The world owes them.

Dishonesty

Toxic people are often deceitful, twisting the truth or outright lying. A dishonest partner might take credit for your achievements or spread false rumours about you to look good. They may be secretive over their phone and emails.

Appointments they go to might be for a totally different reason than they have told you. The messages they're sending may be to someone they know they shouldn't be messaging but they'll say it's their mate or a work colleague. They may cancel time with you on numerous occasions. They simply have something better to do.

Jealous and Envious

They are unable to be happy for others' successes and often try to bring others down. A jealous friend might downplay your achievements or make passive- aggressive comments when you share good news. They'll tell you that you need to relax more. Stop doing so much. and take a back seat

Lack of Empathy

Toxic people struggle to understand or care about others' emotions. An example could be a partner who dismisses your feelings, saying things like, "You're overreacting," or "You're so needy." when you express hurt or sadness. Another one is "Is there something wrong with you?

Controlling

These individuals seek to dominate every aspect of your life, from your social interactions to your decisions. A controlling partner might insist on knowing where you are at all times and get angry if you spend time with others. They'd love to track your whereabouts but watch out if you ever asked to track them in their movements. They always have something to hide.

Gossiping

Toxic people often spread rumours and engage in backstabbing behaviour. A colleague who gossips, might share confidential information or twist facts to damage your reputation. They may disclose your troubles to others whilst over exaggerating everything you're going through.

Unreliable

They frequently break promises and fail to follow through on commitments. An unreliable partner might cancel plans last minute or not show up when you need their support. You can be left standing and waiting as you're dressed ready to go out for a night out. It's soul destroying to say the least.

Passive-Aggressive

Instead of addressing issues directly, they express their anger through subtle digs and sneaky methods that express their negative feelings.. Sarcastic remarks and back-handed comments may not be immediately obvious but you'll pick up on it. A passive-aggressive friend might agree to help with a project but do a terrible job out of spite.

Entitled

Toxic people believe they deserve special treatment and get upset when they don't receive it. An entitled individual might cut in line or demand preferential treatment in group settings. You might be having a conversation and they always revert it back to themselves as the main topic. They want everything their way.

Excessive Drama

This person thrives on creating and sustaining conflict and chaos. A drama-prone friend might blow minor issues out of proportion, creating unnecessary tension and stress.

Inconsistent

Their behaviour and attitudes can change unpredictably, making them hard to trust. An inconsistent person might be supportive, loving and kind one day, then cold and distant the next without any clear reason. They will often disappear out of your life and rock up again a few months later as if nothing has happened. It all depends on their needs and possibly, who's 'Flavour of the Month'. What do they need from you?

Gaslighting

Imagine a scenario where you're certain you've discussed something with your partner, but they completely deny it ever happened. This is gaslighting. A tactic that makes you question your reality and memories, leading to confusion and self- doubt

For example: If your partner claims, "We never talked about that. You must be imagining things," start by keeping a journal.

Documenting conversations can help you trust your memory and provide clarity when things don't add up

When your feelings are dismissed with, "You're being overly sensitive," trust your emotions. Communicate your boundaries.

Narcissism

Narcissism involves an inflated sense of self-importance and a lack of empathy. Narcissists may manipulate situations to keep the spotlight on themselves

If conversations always revolve around your partner, it's important for you to set boundaries to ensure equal sharing time. When your achievements are downplayed, celebrate them with those who genuinely support you.

10 Common Narcissistic Traits

Grandiosity: An exaggerated sense of self-importance and belief in their own superiority.

Need for admiration: Constantly seeking praise and attention from others

Lack of empathy: Inability or unwillingness to recognise or identify with others' feelings and needs.

Sense of entitlement: Expecting special treatment and automatic compliance with their wishes.

Exploitative behaviour: Using others to achieve their own advantage without regard for their feelings.

Envious of others: Believing others are envious of them or feeling threatened by others' success.

Arrogance: Displaying arrogant, patronising or insulting behaviours or attitudes.

Preoccupation with fantasies: Obsession with unlimited success, power, brilliance, beauty or ideal love.

Inability to handle criticism: Reacting with rage, shame, or humiliation when criticised.

Gaslighting: Manipulating others to question their own perceptions and memories.

Not forgetting that a narcissist will always be looking to have a partner that will boost there ego in some way. Often they will line up a new partner whilst you are still in the picture. If they don't get the result they want with the new partner, they will continue to look for a new one that meets their needs. This will be going on whilst you are still in a relationship with them and they remain positive that you are the only one for them

Everyone may display some of these traits occasionally. It's the persistent pattern and intensity of these behaviours that characterise narcissistic personality disorder

Own your successes without relying on the narcissist's approval. If your partner expects constant attention without reciprocation, establish clear expectations for mutual support

Relationships are a two-way street. It's okay to reassess if your needs are consistently ignored. Emotional abuse can be as harmful as physical abuse, Control, isolation and fear are not acceptable

If you're frequently criticised or belittled, the issue lies with the abuser, not you. Engage in positive self-talk and affirm your worth

If you find yourself in a toxic situation, don't hesitate to reach out for support and take steps to protect your well-being. See the resources section at the end of the book.

Emotional Abuse

This often leaves deep psychological scars. Examples below.

Your partner frequently criticises and belittles you, making you feel unworthy.

Abuser: *'You're so useless. You can't do anything right.'*

Recognise that the abuse is about them, not you. Affirm your worth through positive self-talk

Your partner isolates you from friends and family, limiting your support network.

Abuser: *'Your friends don't care about you. You don't need them.'*

Reconnect with your support network discreetly. Explain your situation to trusted individuals who can offer help and encouragement. Consider creating a safety plan if you decide to leave the relationship

Your partner uses guilt to control your actions, making you feel responsible for their happiness.

Abuser: *'If you really loved me, you wouldn't go out tonight.'*

Recognise that you are not responsible for their emotions. Set and maintain boundaries that prioritise your well-being. Assert your right to make independent decisions without guilt or pressure.

By understanding these toxic traits and implementing practical solutions, you can reclaim your power and move towards healthier relationships.

Recognising these traits in people around you can help you set boundaries and protect yourself from their toxic influence. It's crucial to prioritise your well-being and surround yourself with positive, supportive individuals.

You deserve to be treated with respect, empathy and kindness. Toxic people do not deserve a place in your life.

You know the signs. Get those boundaries in place and start to remove these people from your life

It's time to stop picking at your flaws. ignore what others have said about you and move towards a better life

A life where you feel happy and confident.

Chapter 9. Leaving a Toxic Relationship

Leaving a toxic relationship is a critical step towards reclaiming your life and well- being. The process can be extremely challenging and potentially dangerous. This chapter will guide you through the complexities of safely exiting a harmful relationship.

Check out the scenarios below.

Emotional Manipulation and Financial Control.

Sarah's partner, Tom, has systematically eroded her self-esteem over the past three years. He criticises her appearance, intelligence and decisions daily.

Tom controls all their finances, giving Sarah an "allowance" and demands receipts for every purchase. He's gradually isolated her from friends and family, claiming they're "bad influences." Sarah feels trapped, worthless and unsure of how to support herself if she leaves.

Verbal and Physical Intimidation.

Maria's relationship with Alex started wonderfully, but things turned dark. Alex's temper has become increasingly volatile, with frequent shouting matches over minor issues. Recently, Alex has started throwing objects during arguments and making veiled threats like, "You'd better watch yourself." Maria is terrified that the situation will escalate to direct physical violence, but she's afraid of what Alex might do if she tries to leave.

Stalking Behaviour and Refusal to Accept Breakup.

Jennifer ended her relationship with Chris six months ago but Chris refuses to accept it's over. Chris constantly calls and texts Jennifer, sometimes hundreds of times a day. Chris has shown up uninvited at Jennifer's workplace, causing scenes that have put her job at risk. Jennifer has found Chris parked outside her home late at night and suspects Chris might have a spare key. She feels like a prisoner in her own life, constantly looking over her shoulder.

The next part of this book is about leaving a toxic relationship. If you find yourself in a dangerous situation these actions may all apply to you. If not, some may be relevant to you.

Chapter 10. Actionable Steps to Leave

Create a Comprehensive Safety Plan

Identify multiple safe places: Make arrangements with at least two trusted friends or family members who can provide immediate shelter. Research local women's shelters and their policies. Have a backup plan for pet care if needed.

Prepare an emergency bag: Include clothes, toiletries, important documents (Passport, birth certificate, financial records), medication, your phone and some cash. Store this bag somewhere your partner can't find it, possibly with a trusted friend.

Financial preparation: Open a new bank account at a different bank. Start saving money in small increments to avoid suspicion. Research local job opportunities or skill-building programs.

Emergency contacts: Memorise essential phone numbers, including those of your support network, local police, and domestic violence hotlines. Consider creating a code word to alert friends or family of an emergency without tipping off your partner.

Build a Strong Support Network

Confide in trusted individuals: Gradually rebuild connections with friends and family. Be honest about your situation and your plans to leave.

Professional support: Contact a domestic violence hotline for advice tailored to your situation. They can often provide resources you might not be aware of.

Seek therapy: Look for a therapist experienced in domestic abuse. Many offer sliding scale fees or free services. Online options might be safer if you're worried about your partner finding out. See the resources page at the back of this book to talk to me. I have been in your position on more than three occasions.

Join support groups: Consider joining in-person or online support groups for survivors of toxic relationships. Hearing others' experiences can provide validation and practical advice. There are lots on Facebook. See the Resources page at the back of this book. I picked one such group for you.

Document Everything Meticulously

Keep a detailed log: Record every incident of abuse, manipulation or concerning behaviour. Include dates, times and specific details. Store this log somewhere your partner can't access, like a password-protected cloud account. Include police incident numbers if you have any.

Preserve evidence: Save screenshots of threatening texts or social media posts. Record phone calls if it's legal in your area. Photograph any physical injuries or property damage. Ask friends to write the dates and times down if they have been with you during or after the incident

Medical records: If you've sought medical attention due to abuse, you can request copies of your records. These can be crucial for legal proceedings if necessary.

Protect Your Digital Presence and Privacy

Secure your devices: Change all passwords and enable two-factor authentication where possible. Use a password manager to generate and store complex passwords. LastPass is a great app you can use either on your phone or your laptop. It's free and only you can access it.

Check for tracking: Have a tech-savvy friend check your phone and computer for spyware or tracking apps. Consider factory resetting your devices if you suspect they've been compromised.

Create new accounts: Set up new email and social media accounts using a secure, anonymous browser like Tor or Brave. Don't access these from shared devices.

Privacy settings: Review and tighten privacy settings on all your social media accounts. Consider temporarily deactivating or making them private as you execute your leaving plan.

Plan and Execute Your Exit Strategy

Timing is crucial: Plan to leave when your partner is out at work or away for a night, if possible. Have your support network on standby.

Legal protection: Consult with a solicitor especially if you own property and are married.

They can advise you on restraining orders and how to protect your rights.

Inform key people: Let your employer know about the situation, especially if you're concerned your partner might show up at your workplace. Ask about security measures or schedule changes that might help.

Post-exit safety: Change your routine after leaving. Vary the routes you take to work or other regular destinations. Consider staying with friends or in locations your partner wouldn't expect.

Long term planning

Leaving a toxic relationship is a process, not a single event. Once you're out of it, focus on rebuilding your life. Be patient with yourself and prioritise your safety at every step. If you ever feel in immediate danger, don't hesitate to call emergency services. Your life and well-being are precious and you deserve to be safe and respected.

You're going to need to be sly and secretive. Don't even attempt to take everything you own. Material goods are exactly that, material. You don't need them more than you need your sanity, your life and your freedom.

When it's time to go, you'll know. Don't hesitate. There will have been enough time lost. A new start is on the horizon and yours for the taking. Get out while you have the courage.

Life will get considerably better. You will be free to do and say whatever you choose. That's liberating to say the least.

Chapter 11. Personal Stories of Overcoming Toxic Relationships

In my late teens, I found myself stuck in a relationship marked by domestic violence. The man who claimed to love me often turned to aggression, leaving me feeling hurt, bruised, trapped and powerless. I was always walking on eggshells.

At times, I was afraid to utter a single word, just in case.

The breaking point came when I realised that my sense of self-worth had been diminished to the point where I no longer recognised myself. I was sick of bruised ribs and black eyes. With the support of a trusted friend and family members, I plucked up the courage to leave. It wasn't easy. The guy later followed me to another country. He'd found a postcard that gave him a clue to where I would be. It's a long story but I did manage to get rid of him.

Eventually and gradually, I rebuilt my life, rediscovering my strength and reclaiming my identity.

This experience taught me the invaluable lesson that true love is never expressed through fear or control.

Another toxic relationship I endured was with someone who treated me like a doormat, using me for their own amusement while pretending to care.

Despite their declarations of love, their actions showed a complete disregard for my feelings and well-being. The constant emotional neglect took a toll on my self- esteem.

It took time, but I eventually saw through their manipulative behaviour. Through support and self-reflection, I learned to value myself and set firm boundaries.

Walking away from that relationship was liberating and it paved the way for healthier relationships.

I often ask myself why on earth did I attract complete and utter idiots? I'm one of life's helpers. I accept that people are attracted to me for that reason. One thing that is for certain, is that I create my own life. It's up to me who I let in and who deserves to stay.

So, whatever the reasons, lets make a pact right now. Enough is enough.

It's time to stand tall. Stand confident and show ourselves the upmost respect. It is better to be single than to be in a toxic relationship.

There is never any need for us to be so into a guy that he walks all over us and treats us like dirt.

We will walk away, head held high. We are worthy of love, respect and happiness. Lets embrace our strength, cherish our independence and never settle for less than we deserve.

Our future is bright and our potential is limitless. Stand tall and shine on.

If you're at a loose end and not sure where to go from here and a little support wouldn't go amiss, feel free to contact me. The details are on the Resources page.

Chapter 12. Why Positive Affirmations Should Be Your Daily Superpower

Affirmations can seriously change your game: positive affirmations. These little nuggets of self-love are like vitamins for your mind. You need to make them a part of your daily routine.

Firstly, positive affirmations are a quick and easy way to shift your mindset. They help rewire your brain, pushing out those annoying negative thoughts and replacing them with empowering ones. It's like giving your confidence a daily boost!

Secondly, you can do them anywhere, anytime.

Stuck in traffic? Perfect time to remind yourself, "I am capable of handling whatever comes my way."

Getting ready in the morning? Look in the mirror and say, "I am worthy of great things." You don't even need to speak them out loud - silently reciting them works just as well. Make it a habit to sprinkle these affirmations throughout your day.

Start with just one or two that really resonate with you. Say them when you wake up, before a big meeting, or whenever you need a pick-me-up. The more you practice, the more natural it becomes.

Your thoughts shape your reality so by consistently feeding your mind positive affirmations, you're setting yourself up for success, happiness and a more confident you. So why not give it a try? Your future self will thank you!

TODAY IS GOING TO BE INCREDIBLE

I CHOOSE HAPPINESS TODAY

I AM GRATEFUL FOR MY MIND, BODY & SPIRIT

I AM FILLED WITH ENERGY

I AM FULL OF COURAGE & DETERMINATION

TODAY I WILL CHOOSE GREATNESS

MY HEART IS STRONG. MY MIND IS STRONG

I CAN CONQUER ABSOLUTELY ANYTHING

I AM AMAZING

OPPORTUNITY IS EVERYWHERE AROUND ME TODAY

EVERYTHING IS WORKING OUT FOR ME IN THE BEST POSSIBLE WAY

I AM ONE GIANT STEP CLOSER TO MY GOALS

I CAN DO NOTHING I PUT MY MIND TO

I AM FILLED WITH LOVE AND COMPASSION

I AM RESPECTED AND ADMIRED

I AM WORTHY OF MY DREAMS

I AM WONDERFULLY AND BEAUTIFULLY MADE

I AM PERFECT JUST THE WAY I AM

I AM IN TOTAL CONTROL OF MY LIFE

Journaling is a fantastic way to get your thoughts and feelings down on paper. It's a good idea to look back and see how much progress you've made over time.

Answer these questions to make a start.

What are five things that make me happy and how can I incorporate them into my daily routine?

1.
2.
3.
4.
5.

What are 5 negative thought patterns that I tend to fall into and how can I challenge or reframe them?

   1.
   2.
   3.
   4.
   5.

What are 5 things that I am grateful for in my life and how can I create a sense of gratitude on a regular basis?

   1.
   2.
   3.
   4.
   5.

What are some of my strengths and how can I use them to build my confidence?

1.
2.
3.

What are 5 qualities I admire about myself that have helped me through difficult times?

1

2

3

4

5

What are some ways that I can take care of my physical health, such as by getting enough sleep, eating well and exercising regularly?

How has my experience in a toxic relationship taught me about my own strength and resilience?

What does "being the best version of myself" look like to me? How is it different from who I was in my past relationship?

What are some limiting beliefs I've picked up from my toxic relationship that I need to challenge and change?

Who are the positive influences in my life right now and how can I nurture these relationships?

What self-care practices make me feel most refreshed and centered? How can I incorporate more of these into my daily routine?

If I could give advice to my younger self before entering the toxic relationship, what would I say? How can I apply this wisdom to my life now?

What does my perfect day look like?

What do I personally need to work on right now?

Where do I want to be in 5 years time?

How can I start taking steps to achieve this?

About The Author

I'm the big sister of four amazing siblings who had a pretty great childhood. But you know how life throws curveballs? Well, I got hit with a big one in 2004 when I lost my youngest sister. It knocked me for six and I lost my way. I turned to alcohol and cocaine to numb the pain.

Not my proudest moment, but hey, we're all human, right? Even with all that going on, my son gave me a reason to keep pushing forward.

2012 was my year of change. I took the plunge and checked into rehab. Best decision I ever made! Since then, I've not only stayed sober but found my way both in my personal life and my career.

I've been a decorator for over 35 years and after rehab, I added many other skills to my resume. I'm a Life Coach, NLP Master, Holistic Counsellor, Clinical Hypnotherapist and Eye Movement Therapist.

Sounds fancy, but it's all about helping people just like you to overcome their struggles.

These days, I'm rocking the good life! Being a mum and a nan is the best life ever. I use everything I've been through to be there for my family, friends and my clients.

I've been in those dark places, so I get it and I also know there's a way out and I'm here to help light that path.

My story? It's all about bouncing back, growing and changing.

If I can do it, anyone can. I'm just here to show others that no matter how tough things get, there's always hope for healing and success.

So, that's me - Kate May, a former addict turned fantastic mother, daughter, sister and nana and let's not forget the life-changer.

Thank you for purchasing my book. Wishing you all the very best for the future.

Kate xx

RESOURCES

Contact Kate May at

cheltenham-hypnotherapy.com

I offer a range of coaching and therapy services.

Domestic Abuse Helpline:
nationaldahelpline.org.uk Tel: 0808 2000 247

Facebook Groups are a great way to connect with people who may have very similar circumstances.

There were no books used for reference and I have written this book from my own personal experiences and with the knowledge I have learnt whilst training over the last 12 years in life coaching and therapies.

Review Ask

Thank You For Reading My Book!

I really appreciate all of your feedback and

I love hearing what you have to say.

I need your input to make the next version of this

book and my future books better.

Please take two minutes now to leave a helpful review on

Amazon letting me know what you thought of the book.

Thank you.

Kate May

Printed in Great Britain
by Amazon